IDEAS UNLIMITED (PUBLISHING)

© 1993 H Samiy, Ideas Unlimited (Publishing)

PO Box 125, Portsmouth,
Hampshire, UK. PO1 4PP

ISBN 1 87196409 1

Illustrations : Willy Sanker

Limericks : Liz Garrad

Editor : Laurelle D Hill-Dobson

DICATED . . .

TO ALL THE GUYS
WHO WISH THEY HAD
WHAT THEY PRETEND TO HAVE
WHEN IT COMES TO CHATTING UP GIRLS.

Acknowledgement

We would like to thank . . . H R S for his tireles
and persistent research into chatting up, which
went far beyond the call of duty — what a
worker!!

Liz Garrad for her liberally lascivious limericks
which illuminate with levity.

Willy Sanker for his captivatingly candid
cartoons, which elucidate with brevity.

Laurelle D Hill-Dobson for her talent and
experience in Editing.

And, last but not least, YOU the readers,
without whom this book would not be where it

today . . . HERE, IN YOUR HANDS.

An Apology / Warning

We would like to apologise to anyone whose
delicate sensiblities may be offended by
anything contained in this book.

To those of you who have read the above and
have still chosen to read on . . . well,
YOU WERE WARNED!!!!!!

Introduction

To some lucky guys, chatting up girls is second nature (smug sods) but to most of us poor ordinary guys it's a headlong trip into Hell-on-Wheels.

Who do you chat up? Where do you find these girls? How can you tell if she finds you attractive? What can you possibly say to get her attention and even more importantly, to make her like you? What if she's not interested?

Well, before you decide to give up on the whole thing and become a Trappist Monk —

READ THIS BOOK !!!

Contents

Contents

THE CHATUPABLE GIRLS

Half the fun of chatting up for most guys is to show off to their friends how good they are with the girls. In this context girls are divided into two categories.

The first category is the chatupable girls who look georgeous enough for any guy to be seen just talking to them. Talking to such girls even for a few minutes is enough to gain you respect among your friends. If you actually happen to get a "Yes" from her, then you are the KING.

THE UNCHATUPABLE GIRLS

This is the second category of girls. These girls are usually pretty ugly and weird looking. They usually have a great personality and are more loving, sensitive and caring . . . but then again, who cares?

Being seen anywhere near such a girl is bad enough but actually trying to chat her up and failing is such a face shatterer — one which your friends will never forget. To them, you will always be the ultimate loser.

Golden Rule 1 ....

ARE YOU MY KINDA WOMAN?

Unfortunately, in most cases, men do categorise women into the two types described on the previous pages. The type they would love to be seen chatting up and the type they would not want to be seen dead with! Depending of course on their level of desperation, they can occasionally overlook this principle ever so slightly.

> *We're here again, it's Friday night*
> *And I am feeling bored.*
> *It's nearly chucking-out time*
> *And as usual, I've not scored.*
> *All my mates are smooching*
> *And I feel a proper nerd,*
> *One more pint of bitter*
> *And I might ask that ugly bird!!*

Choosing the right person to chat up is a very important rule. Your choice should be based on how your particular character type would harmonise or clash with the character type of your potential prey.

So, just as men can be categorised as specific types (see Chapter 4, "Making the Right First Impression") women can also be grouped into typical categories. It is crucial to know these types, their characteristics, the kind of approach they would welcome and most importantly, the kind of guy who should approach them.

Choose the right person to chat up

Golden Rule 1 . . . .

TYPE 1 : THE SHY, TIMID GIRL

PROS : Sweet nature, grateful for your attention. Very quiet.

CONS : Very quiet.

HER IDEAL MAN : The outspoken life-of-the-party guy. To catch her, you need an easygoing manner, patience and plenty of chat — you'll have to do the talking for both of you!

TYPE 2 : THE SPORTY GIRL

PROS : She can be a VERY good sport.

CONS : Her physical ability may show you up.

HER IDEAL MAN : The fit, healthy, sporty guy (Wimps need not apply). To get her, you will have to exhibit sporting prowess equal to hers — or organise/coach sports events.

Choose the right person to chat up

TYPE 3 : THE CUDDLY GIRL

PROS : She's kind, affectionate and will spoil
you rotten!

CONS : Carrying her over the threshold could be
a problem.

HER IDEAL MAN : A slim guy who loves cuddly
people. To hook her — just ask! She'll be so
grateful you wanted her.

TYPE 4 : THE SHARON TYPE

PROS : Pretty for showing off to your friends

CONS : Insists on talking ocassionally.

HER IDEAL MAN : ANY good-looking guy,
regardless of intelligence or personality). All the
trendy trappings, eg; flash car; cellular phone;
gold chains, are the bait for hooking "Sharon",
she wants 'Flash' not 'Cash'.

3.

4.

TYPE 5 :   THE GOLD DIGGER

PROS : Very easy-to-please (if you have loads-a-money).

CONS : Will screw you for every penny.

HER IDEAL MAN : Anyone who is breathing and has megabucks. Money will keep her.

TYPE 6 :   GIRL GENIUS

PROS : The Thinking Mans' Crumpet. Her conversation will fascinate you. Behind that scintillating intellect, is a passionate nature.

CONS : A hint at your stupidity & you won't see her for dust!

HER IDEAL MAN : A boffin with a body! You'll have to think hard and fast to snare this one and it'll help if you look the part, eg; glasses.

Choose the right person to chat up

TYPE 7 : THE SEX BOMB

PROS : She will quench your every physical thirst.

CONS : Probably your death due to exhaustion! All your friends will be lining up to take your place when you go.

HER IDEAL MAN : Handsome, muscular body, plenty of energy — an ace between the sheets.

TYPE 8 : THE TOMBOY

PROS : She's like one of the guys.

CONS : She's like one of the guys.

HER IDEAL MAN : Someone who likes one of the guys. Find her in your local pub darts team, buy her a pint and treat her like . . . one of the guys.

Golden Rule 2 . . . .

As unbelievable as it may seem to most guys —
women are also from the planet Earth. They
may be a little more complex than the male sub-
species but their signals can still be easily
understood, if observed and interpreted with
skill.

Many good men have had their egos shattered
due to a lack of this skill. They have started to
chat up a girl on baseless assumptions that
she's interested, only to find that she's not!

Unfortunately, by then it is too late . . . which is
why nature has come up with a system whereby
the girl's possible response can be evaluated.
This is, of course, Body Language and most
importantly, Eye Contact.

EYE CONTACT

Research has shown that the information
exchanged between individuals concerning their
emotional and sexual feelings towards each
other is:

	88 %	through the eyes;
	6 %	hearing;
	4 %	sense of smell;
and	2 %	other senses.

If you can master the art of provocative eye
contact, you are home and dry and you don't
even have to smell good!

Eye contact is very important,
Make sure that your gaze never flickers,
A confident stare,
Lets her know that you're there,
And you want to get inside her knickers.

Golden Rule 2 . . . .

Most guys, unfortunately ignore the merits of body language and eye contact. They run around at clubs, pubs and discos trying to chat up everything that moves, completely missing that one girl who has been giving them the come-on all along. This chaotic activity reaches its' maximum speed when the slow dance starts. Then they are really desperate for a "Yes".

So they think that the more they try, the more chances they have of getting that "Yes" . . . WRONG!

The smart guys would take their time, sit down, relax and study the possibilities, constantly looking for the right eye signals to be returned. It is then the time to build up courage and act on the signals received.

> *We've been watching each other for ages*
> *But I can do nothing but stare,*
> *'Cause my Super Glue leaked in my pocket*
> *And my buttocks are stuck to this chair.*

Be sure to read her verbal clues correctly, too — or she'll think you a complete fool.

> *I asked her what she'd like for dinner,*
> *She said "Chateau Briand is fine."*
> *I'm impressed by her,*
> *She's a right connoisseur,*
> *I'd just have any old wine!*

Golden Rule 2 ....

Planning your course of action based solely on eye contact can have its' problems. Certain eye signals can be a little confusing. Have you ever found yourself in a situation where you have spotted a girl giving you a look and a smile, but you still have your doubts as to whether it's a come-on look with the smile of approval, a pity look with the smile of ridicule or even the dreaded hostile look filled with contempt? The insecure guys among you must have noticed this. We now have a Checklist to help you differentiate between 'the intimate look' and 'the hostile look' to save you from either missing a once-in-a-lifetime chance on the one hand or making a complete moron of yourself on the other.

THE RIDICULE GAZE

Unfortunately, for most guys this is the commonest of the three looks. It is, of course, the "Your fly is undone, you idiot." sort of look.

> Our eyes met across the dance floor,
>   I gave her my sexy smile.
> I kept this up almost an hour,
>   To 'let her sweat' awhile.
> At last I sauntered over.
>   I said "Hi, My name's Keith"
> She said "Really? Did you know,
>   You've got cabbage on your teeth?"

THE RIDICULE GAZE

his look is characterised by:

    1) Eyes slightly closed;

d   2) Uninterrupted giggling.

Read her signals correctly

THE HOSTILE GAZE (GET OUTTA HERE)

This is, of course, the second commonest gaze. The gaze which speaks phrases like: "How dare you even contemplate looking at me?" and Come on sucker, make my day. Let's shatter some ego" or even "You spilt your drink on my dress, you imbecile." This gaze can be easily recognised by the following signs:

) the pupils become smaller;
) the eyes open wide;
) the corners of her mouth turn down;
) she frowns;
) following the gaze, she moves her head up or shakes it from side to side, as though she's wondering how you have the nerve to mistake this for an 'intimate gaze';
   and in extreme cases,
) kneeing your groin

THE INTIMATE GAZE (COME AND GET ME)

This gaze is recognisable by the following characteristics:

) the pupils enlarge;
) the eye-lids close slightly;
) mouth slightly open revealing a subtle smile;
) she gazes a little longer than necessary;
   and then . . .
) the head moves down or to one side, pretending it never happened.

THE SIGNALS WHILST CHATTING HER U

Having built up the courage to go over and chat
up the girl you fancy, your task really begins.
You must watch her every move, observe her
reaction to every word you utter. Don't think
that just because she is still sitting there, you
are on to a sure bet.

> *I gazed into her georgeous face,*
> *I even held her hand,*
> *I asked her several questions,*
> *But she didn't understand.*
> *I thought she might be Russian,*
> *Or Polish or a Wop,*
> *Then my fag end brushed her thigh,*
> *And that's when she went POP! !*

The signals you should look for which show that
she is interested are:

if she gazes at you;
if her pupils dilate;
if she straightens her clothing;
if she touches her body or hair;
if she nods her head;
if she moves closer to you;
if she 'mirrors' your posture;
if she 'accidentally' touches you;
if she smiles whilst gazing at you;
if she slips off her shoes/sweater;
if she leans towards you;
if she licks her lips and if she thinks you're very
thick, she may even start to undress . . . THEN
YOU KNOW YOU'RE ON TO A GOOD THING!

Golden Rule 3 . . . .

It's crucial for you to take in as much about her personality as possible right at the start, so that you can improvise and conduct yourself and the chat up in a way which is complimentary to her personality. Her personality and character type can be discovered by noticing her appearance, her hairstyle, her clothes and even what she's drinking

WHAT'S SHE DRINKING?

Cider . . . she's an Easy lady (cross out the 'd'), who likes it cheap and plentiful

A Half of Lager . . . she's probably a Womens Arm Wrestling Champion (approach with caution)

Gin & Tonic . . . she's a Sophisticated Lady, refined and witty

Babycham . . . she'll be your Little Girl Lost;

Straight Spirits . . . she's a real Ball-breaker, better than any man (well, we warned you)

Champagne . . . she'll screw you for every cent (and maybe even then, say "No" between giggles)

Orange Juice . . . she's probably an Alcoholic on-the-wagon (but for how long?)

Perrier . . . she's a Desperately Dieting, Teetotalling, Miss Perfect

White Wine . . . she's a Lady who doesn't drink much or often

Cocktails . . . she's not really a drinker but is trying hard to impress you

PS A womans' attitude to drink reflects her attitude to men. If she's selective about her drink, she'll be choosy about her man — if she'll drink whatever is handy . . ..need I say more?

CHAT UP LINES FOR HEAVY-DRINKERS

I could bore you with my theories,
We could talk about the weather,
But — You like a drink,
I like a drink,
So let's get drunk together! !

HER APPEARANCE : HAIRSTYLES

Hair is the only constant aspect of our
appearance over which we have a great degree
of control. How a girl chooses to wear her hair
reflects her sensuality.

Cropped and Shorn hair is worn by the woman
who . . . does it HER way — OR NOT AT ALL,
the radical feminist.

Short hair is encountered on women who are . .
independent, not overly sensual, modern
careerwomen.

Artificially curled or straightened hair belongs
to a girl who . . . is image-conscious, uncomfort
able with her own nature.

Neat, precise styles are typical of a lady with .
a tightly controlled, repressed sensuality.

Free-flowing, unstyled but clean hair is worn b
a girl who's . . . a free-thinker, uninhibited,
passionate, sensual, natural.

Artificially coloured tresses show a woman wh
. . likes variety and is willing to try new things

HER APPEARANCE : CLOTHES

An untrammelled body, free of overly restrictive clothing indicates a womans' . . . confidence in her sexuality and being comfortable with her own body (and yours, perhaps.)

Tight or buttoned-up or shapeless and baggy clothing that completely covers the body is saying . . .
"Don't touch me" and is demonstrative of repression, strict morality and sexlessness.

Overtly sexy clothing says . . .
'Aren't I georgeous? Sit up and notice me. PAY ATTENTION."

Pastel colours say . . .
'Please take care of me", show a childlike nsecurity, a need to be liked and nurtured.

Bold colours shout . . .
"Look at ME, the person not just the clothes"

Mixed colours and Patterned clothing show her
. discomfort with herself and her body "Who am I?"

Very Fashionable clothing in the latest colours says,she . . . needs the approval and acceptance of others.

Golden Rule 3 . . . .

STAR SIGNS v CHATUPABILITY

ARIES   *"Life is an Exciting Voyage"*

Slender, Sentimental, Feminist, Faithful, Opinionated, Trendy, Self-reliant, Passionate, Possessive, Careerwoman

WATCHPOINT : Potential Ball-breaker

TAURUS   *"Slow and Steady Wins the Race"*

Curvy, Loyal, Highly Sexed, Unpunctual, Stubborn, Dependable, Practical, Sensual, Amiable, Loyal, Party Girl

WATCHPOINT : Not for the guy with a low sex drive

GEMINI   *"Take Me As I Am"*

Bejewelled, Friendly, Outgoing, Micro-Chef, Traveller, Independent, Undomesticated, Sociable, Conversationalist

WATCHPOINT : A better mistress than a wife

Intelligent and witty,
She'll be fickle to the end.
She'll gaze in your eyes
And tell you sweet lies,
While her other hand's groping your friend!

GEMINI

CANCER

CANCER   *"Home is where the Heart Is"*

*raditional, Caring, Sensitive, Committed,
*nsible, Private, Homeloving, Emotional,
*minine, Nurturing, Earth-Mother

ATCHPOINT : Shotgun wedding material

*This girl can be rather possessive,
'Cause she sinks in her claws when she grabs.
When you've had enough,
Getting rid can be tough,
Well, you know what they say about crabs!*

LEO   *"A Star Is Born"*

*erene, Authoritative, Dignified, Exhibitionistic,
*gotistical, Autocratic, Sun-loving, Glamorous,
*nimal-loving, Organiser

ATCHPOINT : Be prepared to be ornamental

VIRGO   *"Do Unto Others . . ."*

*legant, Neat, Undersexed, Precise, Frugal,
*rfectionistic, Selective, Principled, Health-
*onscious, Busy, Intellectual

ATCHPOINT : No sex, no where, no how!

*This girl is obsessively tidy,
She's precise so she won't make you wait.
She keeps her bed neat,
No stains on the sheet,
And her condoms won't be out of date.*

Golden Rule 3 . . . .

LIBRA   *"Variety is the Spice of Life"*

Ladylike, Creative, Loyal, Charming, Poised, Persuasive, Pacific, Refined, Elegant, Sophisticated, Witty, Idealist

WATCHPOINT : Ideal for the flirty and flighty

SCORPIO   *"If a Job's worth doing, it's worth doing well"*

Sexy, Magnetic, Emotional, Ambitious, Hypersensitive, Undomesticated, Analytical, Intuitive, Energetic, Disciplinarian

WATCHPOINT : Can you live in an emotional tornado?

Scorpio is the sign of the Lover,
She'll be generous and pick up your cheques.
She'll bathe you in milk,
She'll dress up in silks,
There's nothing she won't do for sex

SAGITTARIUS   *"What will People Think?"*

Leggy, Ladylike, Adventurous, Sporty, Animal-lover, Intelligent, Religious, Kind, Self-indulgent, Clubby, Gambler

WATCHPOINT : Needs a constant challenge

CAPRICORN *"She who expects nothing will not be disappointed"*

Slinky, Discreet, Ambitious, Loyal, Practical, Professional, Self-Reliant, Logical, Traditional, Resourceful, Tidy, Realist

WATCHPOINT : She won't be Juliet to your Romeo

AQUARIUS *"Freedom, Equality and Brotherhood"*

Egalitarian, Hospitable, Do-gooder, Experimental, Unemotional, Independent, Inconsistent, Ambitious, Intellectual, Individualist

WATCHPOINT : She mighn't fall for your line, but she'll pay for the drinks

The Professor of the Zodiac,
Einstein was one of this bunch.
She can fix any appliance,
She'll blind you with science,
But believe me, this girl's out to lunch.

PISCES *"Seize the Day"*

Sexy, Spiritual, Emotional, Popular, Tolerant, Imaginative, Compassionate, Extravagant, Excitement-seeking, Romantic

WATCHPOINT : She has items in of lingerie which will make your head spin

Golden Rule 4 . . . .

"WOMEN ARE SMARTER THAN MEN"

The quote above is a fact and the sooner guys begin to accept this, the sooner they will be able to plan their moves accordingly and avoid making complete fools of themselves.

When it comes to making a good first impression, most guys fail on the counts of both appearance and character. Even those blessed with the looks to make a good impression ruin it when they open their mouths. Most guys consider themselves to be actors who can play any character they choose. Women, of course, can see right through their pathetic attempts and are left wanting a man who is less like a lavatory — engaged, vacant or full of . . . (claptrap) . . . !!!

THE IDEAL MAN

The qualities which women look for in a man are considerably more varied, individual and personal than the qualities enjoyed by men. A man's ideal woman would have:

          1) Good looks; 2) Good figure;

and   3) the ability to say "Yes".

Women, on the other hand, according to their individual personalities and characters, would find one or more of the following a sign of attractiveness, helping to create that first good impression.

Make the right first impression

HANK HUNKLY

Well, here he is — every womans' Ideal Man . . . Hank Hunkly . . . the guy other men love to hate!!! So, what's to stop YOU from becoming A HUNK.. a guy women lust after and love?

You need to be:
Drop-Dead Georgeous,eg Tall: Strong: Fit: Broad Shoulders: Slender, Firm Waist: Clear, Bright Eyes: Healthy: Muscular Arms, Torso & Legs: Slim Hips: Thick, Clean, Shiny Hair: Long, Shapely Legs: Straight Posture: White, Healthy Teeth: Clear, Smooth Complexion: Small, Firm Bottom.

Hank Hunkly also has such personal qualities as: sincerity; a good sense of humour; warmth; optimism; a caring attitude; the willingness to listen; courage; forcefulness; ambition; protectiveness; intelligence; self-confidence; sensitivity; and last, but not least, Hank is Good In Bed!!!

The following pages present a broad categorisation of men. If you fall into any of these categories, take note and think!

Golden Rule 4 . . . .

PHIL FLASH

Your cellular phone, flashy suit, Stockmarket chat and the big bucks you're making, turn other guys green with envy — but doesn't impress girls!! You're a well-dressed, ambitious guy — not bad, but girls want to know YOU, the person. The trappings of success speak for themselves.

I don't care if you drive a Jag,
I don't care how much money you've got,
I don't want to fly in your Lear jet,
And I don't want to sail on your Yacht.
I don't care if youre a go-getter,
A stock-broker, realtor or banker.
I'm just not impressed, Cause just like the rest,
Underneath all that glitz — You're a . . . BLANKER!

We've shared some conversation,
We've shared a glass of wine,
We've discussed your status,
Your job and your gold mine.
I've heard all your opinions,
You've not heard mine as such,
But according to me,
You've a brain like a flea,
And you fancy yourself FAR TOO MUCH!!

Make the first right impression

SAM SLOB

Okay, Sam, let's talk honestly here. Yes, it's true that the right girl should love the REAL YOU — but the package has to look like it'd be worth unwrapping! Come on Sam, knock 'em out — or could it be you're a little too lazy? If the outside isn't repulsive, she'll want to see the inner you — and you'll avoid replies like these . . .

I can see that you're not on a diet,
And I've heard that you are what you eat,
Tell me, how do you manage with trousers?
It must be hell when you can't see your feet!
I can see that you're such a go-getter,
You don't have the time to bathe,
And when you do, I'm sure that it's true,
You'll probably need a lathe.

No, I can't make it this evening,
'Cause I'm going to fall off my bike,
I'm going to ride straight at some railings,
And end up impaled on a spike.
Yes, I agree it sounds painful.
And instead I could go out with you,
It's a choice between death, And your rotten breath,
So pass me my cycle clips, do!

BOB BOVVER

No man will mess with you unless he has a death wish — but if men are afraid of you, can you imagine the effect your appearance has on girls? If you looked and behaved more like a gentleman than a Caveman, girls would be thrilled by your Macho manliness — once they see that you're not theatening.

I Hate chatting up girls in Disco's,
Having to push my way through the crowd,
And spill half my beer,
Then I shout in 'er ear,
'Cause the music is always too loud.
So I have got a good system,
That cuts out the romantic claptrap.
I yell "Come here luv, quick"
Then I show her my stick,
If she's frigid, then I get a slap.

Make the right first impression

KEV COOL

Hey, Kev — what's happening?

You're such a cool dude and you're so popular with all the other guys who honestly believe you when you tell them that you're Gods' gift to women.

What are you afraid of? Try a little warmth and sincerity and you'll be surprised at the results you get from all those girls who would love to get to know you.

Don't be so indifferent, Kev ... what girl wants to get close to an Iceberg?

You're a real ladykiller, with lines like this one ...

So, what are you doing
on Friday?
There's a crowd going up to
the fair.
It's up to you,
I don't care what you do.
I don't know if I'll even be there.

NORMAN NORMAL

Finally, an ordinary down-to-earth, decent kind of guy. You really are a prize worth winning so let her know it. Get yourself off to a trendy hairdresser (give your barber the Big E) and grab some cool threads. Otherwise, how will she ever know that beneath that nerdy exterior beats a heart of gold? Soon . . .

Let me do your shopping
Let me iron your clothes,
Let me come and kill for you,
Every weed that grows.
Let me clean your windows,
Let me take your calls,
Let me peel a grape for you,
No, I don't mind at all.

Will be... *I'm sorry, I can't date you,*
You'll have to wait in line,
I'm popular of late, Sue,
You'll have to bide your time.
I know you'd love to caress me,
Kiss me and undress me,
But — Oh dear and Bless Me,
You're girlfriend Number 9!!!

Make the right first impression

PETER PITIABLE

It is, of course, not always possible to have all of the qualities mentioned on the previous page and even if you don't have a single one of them — there's still hope. You just need to go around looking as though you need a woman to look after you!!!

Some people say that this brings out the womans' maternal instincts which make you seem attractive to her, but most likely it's PITY.

If you wish to try this route, remember to give them a little incentive, even if it's just a lie at the end of your speech.

> It's Okay, You can walk away,
> Women usually do.
> They think, 'cause I'm not too handsome,
> I must be boring too.
> I've learned to take it like a man,
> When girls have laughed and fled,
> But stick with me
> And you will see,
> I'm dynamite in bed!!

WINNING HER HEART

Surveys have shown that one of the main
reasons for the high failure rate in the field of
chatting-up is the fact that most of the girls
approached have perfect eyesight.

These girls, even if desperate enough to turn a
blind eye to the guys' looks, find it very difficult
to stomach the way some guys present themselves, appearance-wise.

Clothes, hairstyle, jewellery, smell, etcetera are
seen as a reflection of ones' character.

Whichever accessories you choose to wear, make
sure that they are the ones which bring about
the right response.

> *Don't wear a medallion,*
> *You see that's so old hat,*
> *It's just another way to say,*
> *"Ignore me, I'm a pratt."*
> *Don't leave all your buttons undone,*
> *It makes us girls feel sick.*
> *Try rubber tubing down your pants,*
> *That often does the trick.*

Making the right first impression

SMELLS

Don't forget that if the girl of your dreams appears unimpressed by what she sees and not amused by what she is hearing, you could still be in with a chance! Just hope that she is a dog-lover who knows the importance of the sense of smell in choosing a partner.

SUBTLE SMELLS

One problem which could arise from wearing subtle aftershave is that when she comes closer to you, she will see those dreaded hairs sticking out of your nostrils, the hairs you missed when shaving and most embarrassingly, those spots which always come out on Saturdays. So, don't be too sensitive if one of the girls decides to be a little spiteful.

Your spots are quite impressive,
I'll admit I've seen a few.
They must be sad at Clearasil,
'Cause it didn't work for you.
And because you love yourself so much,
It's really quite a sin.
Just come here a tick,
And I'll squeeze them all quick,
If I'm lucky — Your head might cave in!

STRONG SMELLS

A sexy scent is certain,
To bring a woman to her knees.
Calvin Klein, Yves St Laurent,
Try any one of these.
She'll smile and come much closer,
If tempted by the smell,
But just a word of warning,
A fart won't work as well!!

Please remember the effectiveness of wearing aftershave is not measured by how far away people can be and still smell the scent, or by how many people have fainted from its' strength. A good aftershave is most effective when it is subtle enough to make the girl you are chatting up want to get a little closer in order to smell that delicious aroma. If you are so subtle that you don't wear any scent, this could create problems, especially if you spend most of the evening dancing.

You're strutting on the dance floor,
And clearly there's no doubt,
That you think you're ultra-macho,
With your pelvis sticking out.
You don't wear poofy aftershave,
When you take girls for a drink,
But you know, it's quite plain,
When they won't come again,
That you might be a hunk, But you stink!

COMPLIMENTING HER

Complimenting a person usually works wonders
— not only do you get their attention, but you
also let them see that you are a likable person
for liking them.

There are, however, certain guidelines which
must be followed in order to maximise the
effectiveness of the compliment:

1) BE SINCERE

Complimenting someone, just to impress her
enough to get your way or to soften her up for a
favour you want, is an empty gesture. Compliment a girl and then just leave it at that for a
while (this gives her a good impression of you
and marks you out as "not just another guy on
the make"). If it is difficult to be sincere, look
for something you can be sincere about, like . . .
"Isn't that a nice pen you've got?"

2) BE ORIGINAL

Let the compliment be something that she's
never heard before. For instance, for a pretty
girl, you could try: "It's so refreshing to see
beauty and intelligence in such harmony." For a
not-so-pretty girl, you could try: "You're so
pretty."

3) BEAUTY IS IN THE EYE OF THE BEHOLDER

Whatever it is that attracts you to her, will also reveal to her your character. So, if it is her shapely body that you first noticed, she will see that you are only after one thing — if it was the way that her eyes hypnotised you, then you are sensitive and romantic . . .

4) BE CLEVER

Choose your compliments carefully. Make sure that it's a compliment about something which is dear to her heart. It could be one of her passions, hobbies or loves.

5) BE THE EXPERT

A compliment coming from an 'expert' in the field is given much more credit. An optician, for example, commenting on how he's never seen "such beautiful eyes" sounds much better that just anyone saying "You've got nice eyes".

6) BE SWEET

Most girls love romantic compliments, but only if you feel intimate enough for her to take them seriously.

7) CONSTRUCT THE COMPLIMENT TO FIT THE GIRL

Complimenting a girl on something she has done in the past, be it sports or other activities, which you have happened to see, will win her trust and she will believe that other compliments which follow will also be sincere.

Know the way to a girls heart

ROMANTIC COMPLIMENTS

Instead of saying "You look nice — How about
it?" you could try one of these lines.

(WARNING : Before you try these, make sure
that there is a bucket handy for anyone who
may overhear you)

COMPLIMENTING HER FIGURE

*"How many centuries did it take for he who
sculpted you to achieve such perfection of form?
. . . A form, of which, no space is worthy of it's
presence . . . A form, of which, no other form is
worthy of it's company . . . A form, of which, to
touch it is the dream of all other living forms . . .
especially me."*

COMPLIMENTING HER FACE

*"Your eyes are like oceans drowning me for
daring to look into them . . . Your eyebrows are
like canes giving me, the blinded one, hope . . .
Your skin is the soft bed of snow directing me,
your slave, to the glowing warmth of your lips . .
. Lips which conceal the fire of your kiss."*

COMPLIMENTING HER ELEGANCE

*"No man on earth could ever calculate the
equation which has given rise to such elegance .
. Is it the way you glide through the air with such
grace? . . . Is it your beauty which blinds all
creatures? . . . Is it your smile which glows,
putting the sun to shame? . . . Or is it the fact
that you would never refuse the offer of a drink
from a humble creature — like me?"*

THINGS YOU MUST NEVER SAY/TRY ON

Whilst it is true to say that chatting up is an art, it is equally true that it is an art which can be taught, like colouring by numbers. There are certain guidelines which must be followed. In this chapter we will cover the definite "No-No's" when embarking on the art of chatting up.

CHAT UP LINES TO AVOID

"Do you come here often?" This one, as innocent as it may be, could get you into deep trouble.

2) "Hello Darling"

3) "D'you want to have a baby?"

4) "Alright then?"

5) "Hi"

6) "Have you got the time?"

7) "If you've got the time, I've got the money."

8) "Want a drink?"

DO NOT GET TOO CLOSE TO THE TRUTH

I'm afraid a wicked witch,
Has turned me to a frog.
But you could turn me back again,
If we could have a snog!

Golden Rule 6 . . . .

DON'T BE SILLY

Of course it is true that the way to a girls' heart
is through humour. Whilst it is important to try
to be funny, you must remember that certain
things which your friends may find fascinating,
might not go down too well with a girl you've
just met.

You will be successful if you make your girl laugh
So pull a face, tell a joke or trip up on the path.
But there are things you shouldn't do
And you should know this from the start.
As women, we are NOT amused,
To watch you light a fart.

DON'T GET DRUNK BEFOREHAND

It is, of course, necessary for some individuals to
have the odd drink to give them the courage
which they lack in order to attempt to chat up.
However, it is important not to over-do it or else
it could invite disaster.

I admit that I'd had a few lagers,
I was desperate to try and impress,
With the tenth pint I knew I could do it,
It was then I threw up down her dress.

DON'T THREATEN HER

DON'T THREATEN HER

is, of course, very tempting for the guy who has
d a few rejections to try threatening the girl
th taking his own life. I do not believe that
y girl would take such a threat seriously. It
anyhow, a very dangerous idea to try in case
e calls your bluff and gives you a counter-threat.

DON'T BE TOO DIRECT

When you're chatting up,
Try to be subtle,
Take it slowly,
Let her set the pace.
A light touch on the arm,
Will demonstrate charm,
On the tits,
Gets a slap in the face!!!

DON'T APPEAR DESPERATE

Please don't appear to be desperate,
It won't work if you grab her and shout,
"Go on, Give us a kiss,
There's a tenner on this
And without it I can't take you out!"

Golden Rule 6 . . . .

THINGS YOU MUST NEVER SAY . . .

(Because women have learnt to see right
through these remarks)

*"I'm not a sexist or anything . . . but I do believe
that men and women are different."*

*"To me, sex is not that important . . . it's
something that comes naturally."*

"The trouble with women is . . ."

*"What's the matter? Are you frigid or some-
thing?"*

*"I am the kind of guy who respects women and
treats them accordingly."*

*"I hope you don't think that I'm trying to chat
you up or anything, but . . ."*

*"I can't understand women. Why can't they just
be happy with what we men dish out to them and
stop going around with a chip on their shoulders?"*

*"What I look for in a woman is intelligence and
good personality. What she looks like is not that
important to me."*

*"I don't think that men are superior to women .
. there are certain things that women can do
which we men couldn't . . . like having a baby."*

CHATTING UP SOMEONE WHO IS WITH A FRIEND

This is one of the commonest situations in which you are likely to find yourself. The girl you want to meet has come out with her friend. In most cases, these girls would rather meet two guys who are also friends. Trying to chat one of them up on your own is like swimming in a frozen lake - almost impossible. Unless, of course, you can melt the ice.

Make sure that they both like you enough to bring out their sense of competition, thereby creating a 'challenge' to see which one of them gets you.

> *Come on, you know that you want me,*
> *We're both desperate for this date!*
> *But it's me who has to ask you,*
> *You just have to stand and wait.*
> *You're smirking 'cause you're confident,*
> *I'll ask you in the end.*
> *You may be right,*
> *But just for spite,*
> *I think I'll date your friend!*

Be careful, however, not to upset either of them, or else you will return empty-handed.

ne of the ways to a girls' heart is through her
iends' heart. So trying the following line is
ost definitely out!!

> *You've heard this line a hundred times,*
> *From others is my guess,*
> *But you remind me of a famous film star*
> *In that dress.*
> *Standing there with your friend,*
> *It's quite unreal to say the least,*
> *'Cause your friend is quite a beauty,*
> *So you must be the beast!*

inally, if you really feel that she could do
etter than the guy she has been talking to all
ight, try the following line — but be prepared
 case the one who comes over is not her but
he pratt she is dating.

> *Won't you come over and see me,*
> *You'll find that I'm quite fascinating.*
> *Then, I'm sure you'll agree,*
> *That you'd much prefer me,*
> *To that half-witted pratt you've been dating!*

DON'T GET TOO EXCITED

HANDLING THE COMPETITION

Golden Rule 7 . . . .

"WOMEN LOVE THE KISSES
THEY CANNOT GET"

However desperate you are to win a girl over, you must remember that devoting your heart, soul and body to her, to do with as she will (in other words; surgically sticking your lips to her a..) may not always be the right approach.

Appearing to be that catch 'in the bag' may thrill her temporarily, but women, just like men, strive for that challenge. So always leave her guessing as to your intentions whilst appearing to be just a friendly guy.

Playing hard-to-get is a very clever way to get the girls' attention — but it is important to make sure that she has taken the bait and has shown a little bit of interest. Otherwise, it could backfire right in your face.

> *Your beauty is quite breathtaking,*
> *Your charm just leaves me dizzy.*
> *There's little doubt,*
> *That I should ask you out,*
> *But you'll have to wait 'cause I'm busy!*

CHALLENGE HER EGO

On the other side of the coin, we have another approach which has been used in the past with fair amount of success. Namely, the voice of the pitiful guy saying "There's something wrong with me, I can never get passionately aroused." This is a 'dead cert.' particularly with those girl who love a challenge. With such girls, all you need to do then is sit back and enjoy the fruits, but don't let her see that you're enjoying it

> *I'm sure that you find me attractive,*
> *But you're wasting your time, I'm afraid.*
> *Women just throw themselves at me*
> *And at times I have even been paid.*
> *But I just can't respond to your kisses,*
> *They do nothing for me — don't know why,*
> *But if you can't take "No" for an answer,*
> *Go ahead — You're welcome to try.*

WARNING:

It is important not to overdo the above to the extent that she gives up on the challenge and you find yourself back to square one . . . or, ever worse, she may then regard you as that dreaded 'harmless friend'.

Golden Rule 8 . . . .

PRESERVE YOUR EGO

If opening a Greek Restaurant, one would
expect to have the odd plate broken. The same
is true when embarking on the complex world
interacting with the opposite sex, particularly
during the chatting up phase — one should
expect to have the odd ego-shattering experience.

The practice of shattering guys' egos was
started back in 1832 by a group of women
calling themselves the "Ego Shattering Soldier
who held meetings every week in big halls
throughout the country. They were later bette
known as . . . E.S.S. HALLS.

Today this movement is still going strong.
Their ego-shattering lines and verses implante
in womens' minds everywhere.

Apart from their unscrupulous methods of ego
shattering during very innocent attempts at
introduction (the chatting up phase), which we
will cover later, their most enjoyable occassion
is when it hurts the guy most . . . around sex.

They would come up with ego-shatterers such a

"Last time I saw something like that, it was in
birds' beak."

"If this is a race, I guess you just won."

Golden Rule 8 . . . .

"Now that I've had the highlights, can we do the
real thing?"

"How was WHAT for me?"

"Did I come . . . where?"

"You are like B.R . . . always coming but never
getting anywhere."

Don't they realise that men are very sensitive
creatures? Underneath the muscles and the
tough exterior, they are very fragile. A fragile
heart, a fragile mind and a fragile ego.

Having made the effort to go over in an innocent
attempt to save her from the boredom of
loneliness, her first reaction is "Let's shatter
some ego."

We compliment them by telling them that they
are special for having us, with all our qualities,
which we list for them, when chatting them up.

They respond with remarks such as:

We've shared some conversation,
We've shared a glass of wine,
We've discussed your hobbies,
Your job and your Star Sign,
I've heard all your opinions,
You've not heard mine as such,
But according to me,
You've a brain like a pea,
And you fancy yourSELF far too much.

nd then they get really dirty . . .

I don't care if you drive a Porsche,
I don't care how much money you've got,
I don't want to fly in your Lear jet,
And I don't want to sail on your Yacht.
I don't care if youre a go-getter,
A rock star, a jeweller or banker.
I'm just not impressed,
'Cause just like the rest,
Underneath all that glitz, you're a . . .
BLANKER!!!

r they may misunderstand our intentions and
o on about their dirty fantasies . . . !

I've noticed you showing an interest.
I've noticed I'm getting the eye.
You've not yet got around to the chat-up,
But I'm certain you're going to try.
You doubtless think I'm a pushover,
But I'm not the kind who comes cheap.
And if that WERE true,
I still wouldn't date YOU,
I'd much rather French-kiss a SHEEP!!

hen they get really personal with lines like . . .

Tell me, Have you just had surgery?
There's something that looks out of place.
I think you might find,
They've cut off your behind,
And grafted it onto your face!

Golden Rule 8 . . . .

COMBATTING THE EGO SHATTERERS

So, when contemplating chatting up, always take out an insurance policy against damage to your ego. You must be prepared for the worst and have a line prepared to save face.

If the girl who has cruelly rejected you is with another girl, you could say . . .

"Then I guess theres no point asking the pretty one."

OR

"I was talking to your friend."

OR

"Are you girls going steady or just dating?"

If you have just complimented a girl and she's still not fallen for you, you could try:

"I knew it. That line only works when its true."

OR

"I knew it. That line only works on pretty girls."

OR

"Youre the tenth girl to reject that line today."

KNOWING WHEN TO QUIT

The most dreaded moment in any attempt to
chat up a girl is when you are not quite getting
the right vibes. The questions which bombard
the mind are . . .

1.) Is she playing Hard-to-get?
2.) Is she a lesbian?
3.) Should I give up?
4.) Should I start again?
5.) Is anyone watching me?
6.) How can I persuade her?

> *Look, I know you'd like me,*
> *If you'd just give me a chance.*
> *But you refuse to have a drink*
> *And you won't come and dance.*
> *Please — I really fancy you.*
> *I don't do this for fun.*
> *Im desperate — Ill pay!*
> *No, don't go away,*
> *I mean it — Ive got a gun! !*

CHAT UP LINES FOR MASOCHISTS

> *Pleased to meet you, I'm a Masochist,*
> *So go ahead give me some lip.*
> *You can use me, Abuse me,*
> *I don't care if you choose me,*
> *Just give me a crack of your whip!*

Golden Rule 9 . . . .

DOES "NO" MEAN NO?

It is obviously very difficult for a person to know
the various meanings of all the words in the
English language. One particular word is often
misunderstood and judging by the look on some
guys' faces when they hear it, it is a word
they've never heard before. This is, of course,
that dreaded two-letter word "No". Not having
heard the word before, most guys try to
improvise and give the word a meaning
according to the context in which it was spoken.
To these guys:

"NO" means;

"No, I don't want a drink, but please stick
around and chat."

"No, I won't go out with you, but please don't
stop asking 'cause I'm madly in love with you."

"No, I don't want to have sex with you but don't stop
touching me up and forcing yourself all over me."

I guess until such time as we have the meanings of
this word better documented, most guys have to go
through life wishing it never existed or assuming
that it is a word with no specific meaning — like
"an".

> I've told you that "Im busy"
> I've told you "I don't drink"
> I've said "I don't like skating"
> So won't join you at the rink
> I don't want to see a movie,
> Tonight or ANY night.
> Its simple, when I say "Piss Off"
> It DOESN'T mean "I might".

Knowing when to quit

IF ALL ELSE FAILS . . .

There may come a time when you find that, having given it your best shot, your sexiest look, your cleverest chat-up line and all the charm you possess — you are still looking as interesting to her as a fart to a perfumier.

This is the time when you should consider emergency action (a.k.a "Plan Z"). Depending, of course, on the level of your desperation and the fragility of your ego, you could try turning a "No" into a "Maybe" by one of the following;

1) Crying and begging;

2) Shouting and screaming;

or even

3) Creating that sensation closest to her heart.

If options 1 and 2 don't work the 3rd is always a dead cert and it won't be long before she will be putty in your hands and begin uttering those sweet words that are music to every guys' ears.

> *"Yes, I'd love to date you.*
> *Your handsome looks astound me.*
> *'The Chippendales' keep phoning*
> *But I'm glad it's you who found me.*
> *I won't describe you to my friends,*
> *As a boring little git.*
> *You're every womans' dream-come-true,*
> *Now stop twisting my tit."*

OU KNOW IT IS TIME TO QUIT WHEN...

You feel that she may not stop throwing up
r long enough for you to have just one more
y.

She tells you to do a certain four-letter-word
three consecutive sentences.

She physically attacks you for the second
ne.

Her boyfriend, whom she has called over to
scue her, is not the sort of guy that you feel
uld listen to reason.

You hear the first word she has said which
ows the slightest inclination towards wedding
lls.

> *Lust is light-hearted,*
> *No stars in your head,*
> *You buy lots of condoms,*
> *And just stay in bed.*
> *Love can be heavy,*
> *It fills you with gloom,*
> *It costs you a mortgage,*
> *And a honeymoon.*
> *So here's my advice,*
> *Don't start going steady.*
> *Just target a lady,*
> *Who's married already!!*

Golden Rule 9 . . . .

QUICK EXITS

There will always come a time when, having
chatted her up, you feel that something is
missing. Perhaps she wasn't such a challenge,
perhaps it was something that she said that ha
played on your mind.

> *I had spotted her walking 'round Tesco's,*
> *I had gazed at her over the freezers.*
> *She sure had me fooled,*
> *But my passion was cooled,*
> *When she listed her sexual diseases.*

It is at times like this, that you need a quick ex
line. Just saying "Goodbye . . . See you." may n
be genuine enough and might just upset her. T
a line which sounds more honest and believable

> *You're probably not going to believe this,*
> *And I'm sorry I've left it so late,*
> *But I'm afraid that I've got a slight problem,*
> *So I'll just have to cancel our date.*
> *You see, my poor Granny's caught fire,*
> *I don't really know who's to blame.*
> *It might be spontaneous combustion,*
> *But you should see the size of the flame.*
> *I can't leave the poor dear to smoulder,*
> *Next week? Well there could be some doubt,*
> *'Cause I'm sorry to say,*
> *That she's well underway,*
> *And she could take some time to put out.*

Choose the right chat up lines

CHAT UP LINES FOR THE IMAGINATIVE

Just as men are often fed up with getting the same old responses to their chat up lines . . "No" . . . "Sod off" . . . women too get tired of the same old chat up lines. You must therefore try to be original and imaginative to the extent of getting them almost falling for your line or believing you.

Even if you still don't get anywhere, sometimes the trying can still be quite enjoyable. An example of this is the case of the KNEE READER. You have heard of Palm reading and Tea-leaf reading . . . well, meet our Knee reader who convinced three quite leggy ladies that he specialised in knee reading. Starting by telling them a few obvious and true facts, he won their trust and within minutes women were queueing up to have their knees read.

> *I could be like the other guys*
> *Who come over and say "Hi."*
> *But I'd only have to join the queue*
> *And anyway — I'm shy.*
> *So here's an invitation,*
> *To go out with me next week.*
> *You'll be well impressed,*
> *'Cause I'll wear my string vest,*
> *Be prepared — It'll make your legs weak!!!*

Choose the right chat up lines

CHAT UP LINES FOR THE BOLD

It's Okay, I'm a Doctor,
So don't class this as a grope.
I think you may have Poona Crut,
And I'm here to give you hope.
It's a very rare disease,
That affects the larger breast,
Massage is what it responds to,
So don't stop me — I'm doing my best.

Hello, I'm a Genie and your wish is my
command.
I could change your destiny with one wave of
my hand.
I haven't got a magic lamp for you to rub, I fear
But what I've got works just as well,
So slip your hand down here!

I thought about buying you flowers
But it's such a predictable thing.
I thought about hiring a choir
To turn up on your doorstep and sing.
I wanted to do something different,
Something dead snappy and slick.
Then the bright idea came,
I found out your name
And I've had it tattooed on my . . . stick!

Golden Rule 10 . . . .

CHAT UP LINES FOR THE MODEST

I really don't know why I do this,
You're attractive and I'll lose my heart.
You'll lose your head,
Then we'll end up in bed
And that's when the problems will start.
You'll take one look at my body,
Then you'll cry and you'll probably beg.
That's when it will end,
'Cause you won't comprehend,
Just how far my stick hangs down my leg.

CHAT UP LINES FOR IDIOTS

If you're set on failure, go up to her and grin
And say "Pretty please,
May I squeeze,
That huge spot on your chin?"

CHAT UP LINES FOR ELIGIBLE BACHELORS

Can you mend my fuses?
Can you make me laugh?
Can you rescue spiders,
That are lurking in my bath?
Will you tell me jokes,
To cheer me up when I am blue?
If the answer's "Yes",
Then — Marry Me!
I need a girl like you.

CHAT UP LINES FOR THE HUMBLE

Sweetheart, just listen a minute,
And stop trying to put up a fight.
I know that I'm hardly Prince Charming,
And therefore, not your Mr Right,
But I'm decent and honest and generous,
You could at least give me a chance.
Mr Right that you seek,
Might be in here next week,
But I'm here right now — so let's dance.

CHAT UP LINES FOR THE SHY

It took courage to come over here
Because I'm very shy
If you tell me to just go away,
The chances are, I'll cry
But if you come and dance with me,
I'll feel more self assured.
It's probably best
To clutch me to your chest
Then, who knows? After that I'll be cured.

CHAT UP LINES FOR THE SEX MANIAC

How would you like me to,
activate your inner muscles?

If I let you play hard-to-get,
will you let me play to get hard?

Golden Rule 10 . . . .

I've spent the evening watching you
And now I count the cost.
For Cupid fired his arrow
And truly I am lost.
My money's gone on drinking,
While I watched you from afar.
Now I can't afford a Taxi.
Tell me, Have you got a car?

Won't you come over and see me?
You'll find that I'm quite fascinating.
Then, I'm sure you'll agree,
That you much prefer me,
To that half-witted pratt you've been dating!

Golden Rule 10 . . . .

CHAT UP LINES FOR THE HANDSOME

Come on love, 'cause I'm in a hurry,
Five minutes is all that I've got.
Women adore me,
They beg and implore me,
So are you going to shag me or not?

CHAT UP LINES FOR THE ROMANTIC

My lips feel all baggy,
I'm red in the face.
My feet won't keep still
I'm all over the place.
Beer? Whisky? Vodka?
None of the above.
Just — since you walked in here
Well — I think I'm in love!

CHAT UP LINES FOR THE TREKKIE

Would you like to come round for dinner,
It's beef curry for what it's worth.
No, I don't mind . . . you're a Vegan,
That's amazing and Welcome to Earth!

CHAT UP LINES FOR THE DESPERATE

My Mother's washed her hands of me,
My best friend's in a huff,
My boss has just refused my raise,
All in all, my day's been rough.
I'd like to ask you for a drink
But I don't know what you'll say
Give this poor guy a break
Make it "Yes" — For My sake
Go on — MAKE MY DAY. !

CHAT UP LINES FOR THE GENEROUS

I'd do anything for you,
Your wish is my command.
I'll deck you out in diamonds,
Or hire a big brass band.
I would be delighted,
To date a lady of your class.
So dine with me,
And you will see,
I'm great at Kissing . . . Lass!

CHAT UP LINES FOR THE TIGHTFISTED

I should offer you Champagne and oysters,
Dinner and maybe a show,
But I couldn't risk it,
So here — Have a biscuit
And a nice glass of fresh H20.

Golden Rule 10 . . . .

CHAT UP LINES FOR THE ORIGINAL

First, select your victim. Go up to her and say "May I just take the ice out of your drink?". Do so and then crush it under your heel. Now say "Now that we've broken the ice, I'm . . . X . . ."

CHAT UP LINES FOR SHORT GUYS

I'm not that successful with women,
It's got something to do with my height.
Pleased to meet you, My name is Gropy
And I'm hoping that yours is Snow White.

CHAT UP LINES FOR UGLY GUYS

It's true that no-one is this ugly.
I'll point that out first, should you ask.
But please feel quite free,
To sit on my knee
And then, I might take off the mask.

CHAT UP LINES FOR THE NOT-SO-INTELLIGENT

I asked her what she'd like for dinner,
She said "Chateau Briand is fine."
I'm impressed by her,
She's a right connoisseur,
I'd just choose any old wine.

HAT UP LINES FOR THE ORIGINAL

Some men buy flowers on impluse,
Some fall in love, So it's said.
But I thought you might care,
For my old Teddy Bear.
We're inseparable — Take us to bed!

Golden Rule 10 . . . .

CHAT UP LINES TO TRY ON APPROACHABLE GIRLS

You've flattered me 'till I'm quite breathless,
You've kissed me and plied me with booze.
Now you've produced flavoured condoms,
No, I've go no preference, You choose!

CHAT UP LINES TO TRY ON SEXY-REVEALING-DRESSED GIRLS

I'm sorry and distressed,
'Cause you caught me staring,
But I love that dress
You're nearly wearing.
I've watched you dance the night away,
And I think it only fair,
To tell you that the seam has split
And your buttocks are all bare.

CHAT UP LINES TO TRY ON VERY PRETTY GIRLS

Tell me, Is it really true,
Or is it just a rumour?
That girls who look as good as you,
Have got not sense of humour?
You can't have too much trouble,
When it comes to guys and scoring,
But if you won't come out with me,
Then I was right — You're Boring!!

CHAT UP LINES TO TRY ON THE UNAPPROACHABLE GIRL

You're really quite hard to get close to,
I know, I've been trying all night.
So, give us a smile,
I'm stood back half a mile,
By the way, Does that Rottweiler bite?

CHAT UP LINES TO TRY ON THE UGLY GIRLS

You see that georgeous girl over there,
She's just been really hateful.
She meant it, too,
So I'll chat to you . . .
At least your sort are grateful.

CHAT UP LINES TO TRY ON OLDER-LOOKING GIRLS

Hello, I thought you looked lonely,
Is this disco a bit of a bore?
Move closer, my dear,
And I'll shout so you'll hear,
Tell me, What did you do in the War?

CHAT UP LINES TO TRY ON ANGRY-LOOKING GIRLS

Blimey, Has someone upset you?
You look really fierce when you frown.
Do you want a job?
You could earn a few bob,
'Cause we've just had our Pit-bull put down.

CONVERSATION OPENERS / ICE BREAKERS

"Have you noticed how the people here are all s
friendly?"

Select your victim. Go up to her and say "May I
just take the ice out of your drink? Do so, then
crush it under your heel. Then say "Now that
we've broken the ice, I'm . . . X . . . "

"You know, sometimes I feel ashamed of being a
man — like when I see all these guys pouncing
on girls and trying to chat them up and ending
up just making a nuisance of themselves."

"It's good to see that there are more girls than
guys here tonight. That means that when you
see an intelligent girl you want to talk to, she's
not being chatted up by three guys at once."

"Excuse me, but I've never been here before . . .
Why are all these guys wandering around
talking to different girls, then walking away
when they shake their heads??? . . . They're
doing WHAT??? . . . WHAT IDIOTS!!!"

"You know what they should do here to encour-
age more intelligent conversation? They should
only allow people in here with paper bags over
their heads. That way, maybe guys would forge
about sex for awhile and try to find out what th
girls are like as human beings."

CHAT UP LINES FOR THE BLIND

I'm sorry, I'm partially sighted,
But if I hear you and touch you, you're real,
So come closer, my dear,
And whisper in my ear,
While I have a bit of a feel.

Golden Rule 10 . . . .

CHAT UP LINES FOR GIRLS

We must dedicate a few pages to those poor
girls who spend hours giving out all their
sexiest 'come on' signals to that special guy,
only find that he is either too blind or too stupid
to read subtle signals.

Look! We're in the 90's now,
So give a girl a break,
Do I really have to wait
For you — for goodness sake!
I'd really like to dance with you
To something nice and slow,
So here's a card to tell you,
There, I've said it,
Now you know!

I'd really like to dance with you,
And here's a card to tell you,
I could identify your aftershave,
If I had the chance to smell you.
So when things are slowing down a bit,
Will you have a dance?
Who knows? You may be boring,
But I'm brave — I'll take the chance!

A point of warning to any guy who sees the girl
come over to talk. Don't jump to conclusions . .

It's not unusual for girls to chat guys up,
So I hope this request won't offend,
But do you think,
You could just hold my drink?
'Cause I'm eager to talk to your friend!

Golden Rule 10 . . . .

CHAT UP LINES (ON A CARD) FOR THE SHY

There will always be occasions when you feel
that, considering the circumstances, it would be
better to chat up the girl of your dreams via
remote control. You may be very shy or just not
quite at your best at that time.

It is at times like this that a little chat up line
message sent to her, perhaps with a single
flower, would do the trick. Her curiousity to find
out her secret admirer coupled with her sense of
play would both work in your favour. You must
remember to note down your telephone number
for her to contact you — but keep her guessing
for as long as you can.

Depending on the situation at hand, you could
use one of the following:

> *I agree, this is a novel way,*
> *By which to ask you out,*
> *If I did this the proper way,*
> *You'd turn me down, no doubt.*
> *So just fill in this questionnaire,*
> *It isn't very hard.*
> *Just place your tick by yes or YES,*
> *And hand me back this card.*

Choose the right chat up lines

My body's gone to pieces,
My mind is in a whirl
And I can see from here that,
You're a most outstanding girl.
I'd really like to rub some,
Sun-tan oil into your back.
I'd like to come and ask you.
It's not confidence I lack.
But I've noticed your bikini
And it's truly double-breasted
And if I get up to walk right now,
I'll no doubt be arrested!!
So will you meet me later
And perhaps we'll do the town?
I'll be back in an hour,
When I've had a cold shower,
To see if it helps things calm down!

My name is.................................
It's written down so don't forget it,
My numbers here too,
Now it's all up to you.
Call me, you'll never regret it.

CHAT UP CARDS

Do you dance 'round your handbag?
Do you only go out at weekends?
Do you stand in the corner and giggle?
And go off to the loo with your friends?
I hope you'll take part in this survey,
You'll find my 'phone number above.
If the answer is "No" to all questions,
Then, call me — This could be true love!

My Granny always gave advice
And this is what she said,
"You can't expect young girls,
To just leap into bed."
So this invitation card
Invites you for a drink,
'Cause it's always best,
To start off well refreshed,
That's what I think!

CHAT UP CARDS

Can you mend a faulty fuse?
Can you make me laugh?
Can you rescue spiders
That are lurking in my bath?
Can you cheer me up
With dirty jokes when I am blue?
If the answer's "Yes",
Then, Call me up
I need a girl like you!

Girls don't seem to like me,
It makes me feel quite humble,
They don't seem to understand me,
But that's because I mumble.
I hope that you are different
And you'll have a little pity
And if you still won't call me
Well, I hope you like this ditty.

CHAT UP CARDS

I wanted to spark off your interest,
So that you would come out for a drink,
But I can't think of a thing,
What's your number? I'll ring,
And be witty, when I've had a think.

I'd really like to talk to you,
But you'd never hear a thing.
So will you take my number,
And perhaps give me a ring?
I could just stand next to you,
And bellow in your ear
But you're too good for that
And I'd feel like a pratt,
So call me, We'll go for a beer.

Choose the right chat up lines

CHAT UP CARD

Cut out this card and give it to that special girl.

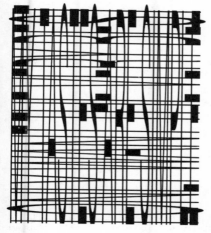

To find out the message contained in the above and how to read it, please turn over the page.

CHAT UP CARD

To read the Special Message Puzzle on the previous page:
1) Hold the card up to just below eye level, as though you
were going to look at something else over it;
2) Angle the far edge of the paper downwards away from
you, so that the writing appears to be only 1/2 inch high;
3) The message can now be read easily.
There are two parts to this message, for which you will need
to read from two sides of the page.
The message on this card is . . .
    "My tastes are simple: I only want the very best."

Choose the right chat up lines

CHAT UP CARD

Cut out this card and give it to that special girl.

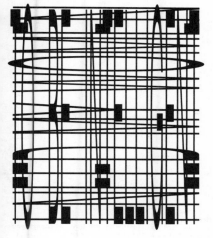

To find out the message contained in the above
and how to read it, please turn over the page.

Golden Rule 10 . . . .

CHAT UP CARD

To read the Special Message Puzzle on the previous page:
1) Hold the card up to just below eye level, as though you
were going to look at something else over it;
2) Angle the far edge of the paper downwards away from
you, so that the writing appears to be only 1/2 inch high;
3) The message can now be read easily.
There are two parts to this message, for which you will need
to read from two sides of the page.
The message on this card is . . .
    "I need my women : To be intelligent."

Choose the right chat up lines

CHAT UP CARD

Cut out this card and give it to that special girl.

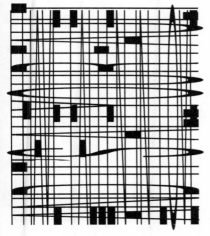

To find out the message contained in the above
and how to read it, please turn over the page.

CHAT UP CARD

To read the Special Message Puzzle on the previous page:
1) Hold the card up to just below eye level, as though you
were going to look at something else over it;
2) Angle the far edge of the paper downwards away from
you, so that the writing appears to be only 1/2 inch high;
3) The message can now be read easily.
There are two parts to this message, for which you will need
to read from two sides of the page.
The message on this card is . . .
"I have fallen in love : And it's all your fault."

CHAT UP CARD

ut out this card and give it to that special girl.

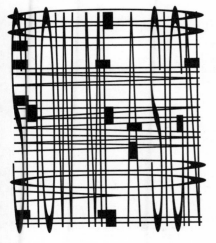

To find out the message contained in the above
and how to read it, please turn over the page.

| CHAT UP CARD |

To read the Special Message Puzzle on the previous page:
1) Hold the card up to just below eye level, as though you were going to look at something else over it;
2) Angle the far edge of the paper downwards away from you, so that the writing appears to be only 1/2 inch high;
3) The message can now be read easily.
There are two parts to this message, for which you will need to read from two sides of the page.
The message on this card is . . .

"If you want me too: show me a sign."

---

hoose the right chat up lines

CHAT UP CARD

t out this card and give it to that special girl.

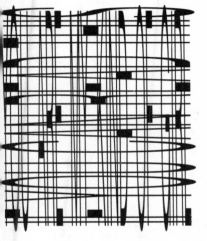

'o find out the message contained in the above
and how to read it, please turn over the page.

Golden Rule 10 . . . .

CHAT UP CARD

To read the Special Message Puzzle on the previous page:
1) Hold the card up to just below eye level, as though you were going to look at something else over it;
2) Angle the far edge of the paper downwards away from y̶ so that the writing appears to be only 1/2 inch high;
3) The message can now be read easily.
There are two parts to this message, for which you will nee̶ to read from two sides of the page.
The message on this card is . . .

"If you can read this : You are my kind of girl."

TITLES AVAILABLE FROM IDEAS UNLIMITED (PUBLISHING)

Please send me (Postage free)

❑ copies "100 CHAT UP LINES"
ISBN: 1 871964 00 8 (128 pages A7)   @ £1.99

❑ copies "THE IDIOTS' HANDBOOK OF LOVE & SEX"
ISBN: 1 871964 08 3 (128 pages A7)   @ £1.99

❑ copies "WELL HUNG" (Full Colour)
ISBN: 1 871964 07 5 (96 pages A5)   @ £2.99

❑ copies "BODY LANGUAGE SEX SIGNALS
ISBN: 1 871964 06 7   (64 pages)   @ £2.50

❑ copies "OF COURSE I LOVE YOU"
ISBN: 1 871964 01 6 (96 pages A6)   @ £1.99

❑ copies "THE BEGINNERS GUIDE TO KISSING"
ISBN: 1 871964 02 4 (64 pages A5)   @ £2.50

❑ copies "TIPS FOR A SUCCESSFUL MARRIAGE"
ISBN 1 871964 03 2 (64 pages A5)   @ £2.50

❑ copies "THE JOY OF FATHERHOOD"
ISBN: 1 871964 04 0 (64 pages A5)   @ £2.50

❑ copies "OFFICE HANKY PANKY"
ISBN: 1 871964 05 9 (64 pages A5)   @ £2.50

❑ copies "10 GOLDEN RULES OF CHATTING UP"
ISBN: 1 871964 09 1 (128 pages A7)   @ £1.99

Please see over for Order form.

I have enclosed a cheque/ postal order for
£...................................... made payable to
Ideas Unlimited (Publishing).

NAME: ———————————————————

ADDRESS: ————————————————

————————————————————————

————————————————————————

COUNTY:————— POST CODE: ————

Fill in the coupon above and send it with your
payment to:

        Ideas Unlimited (Publishing)
        PO Box 125
        Portsmouth
        Hampshire PO1 4PP

Postage free within the United Kingdom.

If you wish your purchase to be sent directly to
someone else (eg: a Birthday / Christmas /
Wedding / Valentines gift), simply fill in their
name and address in the coupon above and
enclose your cheque/postal order, with your
personal message or card, if desired. We will be
pleased to send your gift directly to your chosen
recipient.

I have enclosed a cheque/ postal order for
£..................................... made payable to
Ideas Unlimited (Publishing).

NAME:_____

ADDRESS:_____

_____

_____

_____

COUNTY:_____ POST CODE:_____

Fill in the coupon above and send it with your
payment to:

        Ideas Unlimited (Publishing)
        PO Box 125
        Portsmouth
        Hampshire PO1 4PP

Postage free within the United Kingdom.

If you wish your purchase to be sent directly to
someone else (eg: a Birthday / Christmas /
Wedding / Valentines gift), simply fill in their
name and address in the coupon above and
enclose your cheque/postal order, with your
personal message or card, if desired. We will be
pleased to send your gift directly to your chosen
recipient.